Rookie
Read-About® Safety

Bicycle Safety

by Lisa M. Herrington

Content Consultant
Debra Holtzman, J.D., M.A.

Reading Consultant
Jeanne Clidas, Ph.D.
Reading Specialist

Children's Press®
An Imprint of Scholastic Inc.
New York Toronto London Auckland Sydney
Mexico City New Delhi Hong Kong
Danbury, Connecticut

Dear Parent/Educator:

It is very important that children learn how to be safe when riding a bicycle. However, this is something they might need help with from a grown-up. If your child needs that help, we hope you will use this book as a springboard to a discussion about bicycle safety with him or her. You can read the book together the first time, and talk about the different suggestions inside.

Library of Congress Cataloging-in-Publication Data
Herrington, Lisa M.
Bicycle safety / by Lisa M. Herrington.
  p. cm. — (Rookie read-about safety)
 Includes index.
 ISBN 978-0-531-28968-6 (library binding) — ISBN 978-0-531-29270-9 (pbk.)
 1. Cycling—Safety measures—Juvenile literature. 2. Bicycles—Safety measures—
Juvenile literature. I. Title.
 GV1055.H47 2012
 796.6—dc23   2012013377

Produced by Spooky Cheetah Press

Photographs © 2013: age fotostock/Tono Balaguer: 24; Alamy Images/Bilderbox/
INSADCO Photography: 28; iStockphoto/Marilyn Nieves: 11; Keith Plechaty: 10;
Media Bakery: 15 (Sandro Di Carlo Darsa), 27 (Somos); PhotoEdit: 16, 20 (David
Young-Wolff), 19, 22, 23 left, 23 right (Michael Newman); Thinkstock: 3, 31 top left,
31 bottom left, 31 bottom right (Hemera), 4, 8, 12, 31 top right (iStockphoto), cover
(Jupiterimages), 7 (Stockbyte/altrendo images).

Table of Contents

Safe Riding

Riding a bicycle is fun! It also keeps your body healthy. Learn how to be a safe rider.

Pick a bike that is the right size for you. It should have reflectors and a bell or a horn.

Wear the Right Gear

Always wear a helmet. It will protect your head when you fall.

Your helmet should sit straight on your head and be snug under your chin. If your helmet moves, it is not on right.

**too far
forward**

**too far
back**

perfect

Wear bright colors when you ride. Drivers need to be able to see you.

Do not ride at night. It is hard for drivers to see you in the dark.

Rules of the Road

Kids should ride on the sidewalk or on a bike path. Stop at every corner. Get off your bike and walk it across the street.

Follow traffic rules
just as cars do. Obey
traffic signs and lights.

If you have to use the street, ride on the right side of the road. Look out for bumps and potholes.

Look behind you
before turning.
Always use hand
signals.

right turn

left turn

stopping

Do not wear headphones when you ride. You need to hear what is going on around you.

Expect the Unexpected

Watch out! Cars can quickly turn in front of you or pull out of driveways. Ring your bell or honk your horn to let people know you are there.